PREHISTORIC WORLD

THE ICE AGE

Dougal Dixon

Copyright © 2006 *ticktock* Entertainment Ltd. First published in Great Britain by ticktock Media Ltd.,
Unit 2, Orchard Business Centre, North Farm Road, Tunbridge Wells, Kent TN2 3XF, Great Britain.

A CIP catalogue record for this book is available from the British Library.

ISBN 1 84696 037 1

Printed in China

CONTENTS

INTRODUCTION

This map shows how the Earth looked in the Quaternary Period. The white areas show how much of the Earth was covered in glaciers.

This map shows how the Earth looks today. It does not look very different from the continents in the Quaternary Period.

Prehistoric World is a series of six books about the evolution of animals.

The Earth's history is divided into sections called periods. These periods last millions of years. Each book in this series looks at the most important periods in prehistory.

This book looks at the Quaternary Period, when an ice age took hold of Earth. New animals evolved which could survive the harsh weather. By the end of this period our human ancestors started to appear.

PREHISTORIC WORLD TIMELINE

Use this timeline to trace prehistoric life. It shows how simple creatures evolved into more different kinds.
This took millions and millions of years. That is what MYA stands for – millions of years ago.

	BOOK	PERIOD	
CENOZOIC ERA	**THE ICE AGE**	1.75 MYA to now QUATERNARY	This is a period of ice ages and mammals. Our direct relatives, Homo sapiens, also appear.
	ANCIENT MAMMALS	65 to 1.75 MYA TERTIARY	Giant mammals and huge, hunting birds appear in this period. Our first human relatives also start to evolve.
MESOZOIC ERA	**CRETACEOUS LIFE**	135 to 65 MYA CRETACEOUS	Huge dinosaurs evolve. They all die by the end of this period.
	JURASSIC LIFE	203 to 135 MYA JURASSIC	Large and small dinosaurs and flying creatures develop.
	TRIASSIC LIFE	250 to 203 MYA TRIASSIC	The 'Age of Dinosaurs' begins. Mammals also start to appear.
PALAEOZOIC ERA	**EARLY LIFE**	295 to 250 MYA PERMIAN	Sail-backed reptiles start to appear.
		355 to 295 MYA CARBONIFEROUS	The first reptiles appear and tropical forests develop.
		410 to 355 MYA DEVONIAN	Bony fish evolve. Trees and insects appear.
		435 to 410 MYA SILURIAN	Fish with jaws develop and land creatures appear.
		500 to 435 MYA ORDOVICIAN	Primitive fishes, trilobites, shellfish and plants evolve.
		540 to 500 MYA CAMBRIAN	First animals with skeletons appear.

MEGALANIA

When the first people arrived in Australia 40,000 years ago, they must have been terrified by *Megalania*. This gigantic lizard was the size of a lion. It was a fierce predator, with sharp teeth and big claws. It would have hunted by ambush, lying in wait until its prey came close, then leaping out to attack.

Megalania may have hunted in short bursts of speed. It would not have been able to run fast for long. Like other reptiles, *Megalania* could not control its body temperature, and so it would have over-heated if it tried to run too fast for too long.

Scientists have not yet found a full skeleton of *Megalania*. The individual bones that have been found suggest that it had quite a short tail, and a massive body.

ANIMAL FACTFILE

NAME: *Megalania* (great ripper)

PRONOUNCED: meg-al-ai-nee-ah

GROUP: Varanid lizard

WHERE IT LIVED: Australia

WHEN IT LIVED: Early Quaternary Period (1.6 million to 40,000 years ago)

LENGTH: 5.5 metres

SPECIAL FEATURES: The biggest lizard that has ever existed

FOOD: Meat, either from animals it caught itself, or scavenged from the bodies of those that were already dead

MAIN ENEMY: Carnivorous marsupials, such as *Thylacoleo*

DID YOU KNOW?: *Megalania* would have tackled prey up to ten times its own weight. That means that it could have hunted the biggest animals in Australia at that time.

DINORNIS

Before early people reached New Zealand, about 1,000 years ago, bats were the only mammals living there. However, there was a vast range of ground-dwelling birds known as the moa. The biggest of these was *Dinornis*. It was the largest bird to have ever lived.

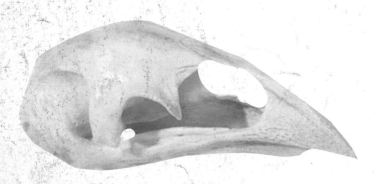

When you see a moa skeleton in a museum, it often has its head held high. In life it would usually have held its head close to the ground, where the food was. It would have looked up to scan for danger.

During the Quaternary Period, New Zealand was covered in forest. *Dinornis* had a short, broad beak. It was ideal for rooting about in thick forest undergrowth to find the tastiest food.

ANIMAL FACTFILE

NAME: *Dinornis* (terrible bird)

PRONOUNCED: die-nor-nis

GROUP: Ratite – flightless birds

WHERE IT LIVED: New Zealand

WHEN IT LIVED: Throughout the Quaternary Period (1.6 million to 200 years ago)

HEIGHT: 2 metres at the mid-point of the back

SPECIAL FEATURES: Giant flightless bird with a tiny head and enormous legs

FOOD: Twigs, berries and leaves. It also swallowed stones to help to grind up the food

MAIN ENEMY: People, and a kind of giant eagle that lived in New Zealand

DID YOU KNOW?: There were 11 different species of moa, some only the size of a turkey. Humans hunted moas to extinction a few hundred years ago.

THYLACOLEO

Most of the mammals of Australia are marsupials – they carry their young in pouches. Today there are marsupials that are tree climbers (koalas), grass-eaters (kangaroos), and burrow-dwellers (wombats). In the Quaternary Period there was a marsupial version of the lion – *Thylacoleo*.

The strong front legs and the big claw on the thumb of *Thylacoleo* suggest that it ambushed its prey. It would have waited in overhanging branches until it could leap down, wrestling its prey to the ground and killing it by slashing and biting.

The muscle attachments on the jaws of *Thylacoleo* show that it would have produced the strongest bite of any known mammal. Its bite was about the same as an African lion – although it was half its size.

ANIMAL
FACTFILE

NAME: *Thylacoleo* (pouched lion)

PRONOUNCED: thy-lac-oh-lee-oh

GROUP: Marsupial mammal

WHERE IT LIVED: Australia

WHEN IT LIVED: Late Tertiary Period to the Early Quaternary Period (24 million to 30,000 years ago)

LENGTH: 1.2 metres

SPECIAL FEATURES: Killing teeth at the front and huge meat-shearing teeth at the back

FOOD: Big marsupial mammals

MAIN ENEMY: None

DID YOU KNOW?: Some scientists thought that *Thylacoleo* was a plant-eater, and that the big teeth were for splitting hard fruit. Most now agree that it was a meat-eater.

MEGATHERIUM

A sloth today is a little animal, and the biggest is about as large as a medium-sized dog. It hangs upside down from trees and nibbles leaves. In prehistoric times, some sloths were the size of elephants. They were much too big to live in trees. They had huge claws that could rip away at branches, and pull down high trees to feed. *Megatherium* was the biggest of these ground sloths.

This skeleton of *Megatherium* shows it had broad hip bones and massive hind legs. It probably sat, as solid and stable as a pyramid, while reaching up to snatch leaves and twigs from the trees.

NAME: *Megatherium* (great beast)

PRONOUNCED: meg-ah-theer-ee-um

GROUP: Xenarthran mammal

WHERE IT LIVED: South America

WHEN IT LIVED: Early to Mid Quaternary Period (1.9 million to 8,000 years ago)

LENGTH: 6 metres

SPECIAL FEATURES: Huge claws on front and hind feet, shaggy fur

FOOD: Shoots and leaves, but some scientists think that the big claws may have meant that they were meat-eaters

MAIN ENEMY: Carnivorous mammals such as *Smilodon*

DID YOU KNOW?: In the 19th century there was a theory that the first people farmed *Megatherium* by walling them up in caves. We now know that the animals had been trapped naturally, by rock falls.

The first people in South America hunted these great creatures for food. There would have been enough meat on a *Megatherium* to feed a whole tribe.

DOEDICURUS

Doedicurus looked like an armadillo but was the size of a car. The glyptodonts evolved in South America in Early Quaternary times, while the continent was still an island.

Doedicurus was shaped like most of the other glyptodonts, but it had a fearsome, spiked club on the end of its tail.

Doedicurus had solid armour made of small pieces of bone joined together. Around the joints, there were gaps between the pieces to make the armour flexible – like chain mail.

The tail of *Doedicurus* was stiff and straight. The only place it could be bent was at the base, which made it very strong. It would have been swung with great force from the powerful hips.

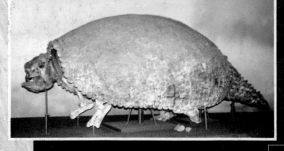

MEGALOCEROS

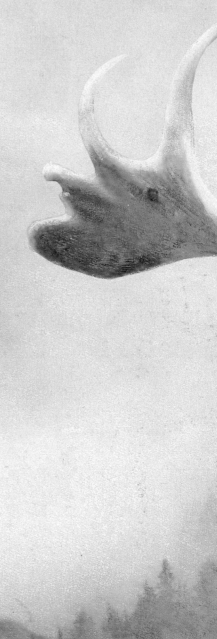

Modern moose and elk have spectacular antlers. However, these are tiny compared with the antlers of the big Ice Age deer *Megaloceros*. Each antler would have been about 1.5 metres – longer than you are! Only male deer had antlers. They used them to attract a mate and fight off rivals.

Megaloceros lived in many European countries, but it was particularly common in Ireland, where there were no predators and plenty of food. The antlers of *Megaloceros* are often found in Irish peat bogs. For this reason, it is also known as the Great Irish Elk.

The leader of the *Megaloceros* herd must have been a magnificent sight, watching over his herd and protecting it against other males. However, he could not guard against the hunting skills of early humans. By the end of the Ice Age it was hunted to extinction.

ANIMAL
FACTFILE

NAME: *Megaloceros* (giant horn)

PRONOUNCED: meg-ah-loss-er-oss

GROUP: Artiodactyl

WHERE IT LIVED: Europe and Western Asia

WHEN IT LIVED: Mid Quaternary Period (1.5 million to 11,000 years ago)

HEIGHT: 3 metres

SPAN OF ANTLERS: 3.3 metres. Today, the largest moose antlers have a span of about 2 metres

SPECIAL FEATURES: Enormous antlers that were shed and regrown every year

FOOD: Grass and low-growing vegetation

MAIN ENEMY: Early humans

DID YOU KNOW?: *Megaloceros* needed large amounts of minerals to grow its antlers every year. About 11,000 years ago the climate became colder and the vegetation that provided these minerals became less common. Climate change, together with hunting by early humans, led to *Megaloceros'* extinction.

MAMMUTHUS

Probably the most familiar of the Ice Age
mammals is the woolly mammoth, with
its long shaggy hair and massive curved
tusks. Unlike today's elephants that
live in hot countries, the mammoth
was adapted to the cold.

Sometimes mammoths became buried in mud when they sank into a peat bog, or when a riverbank collapsed on them. This mud later froze. As a result, we sometimes find complete frozen bodies of mammoths, thousands of years old.

The thick hair of the mammoth protected it from the cold. The hump on its shoulders contained a food supply of fat that would see it through the harsh winters. The huge curving tusks were used as snowploughs, for scraping snow away from the mosses, lichens and grasses on which it fed.

ANIMAL FACTFILE

NAME: *Mammuthus* (burrowing one)

PRONOUNCED: mam-eth-us

GROUP: Elephantidae

WHERE IT LIVED: Canada, Alaska, Siberia and Northern Europe

WHEN IT LIVED: Late Tertiary Period to Late Quaternary Period (4.8 million years ago to 2,500 years ago)

HEIGHT: 2.7 metres at the shoulders

SPECIAL FEATURES: Adaptations to living in a cold climate

FOOD: Grasses, lichens and mosses

MAIN ENEMY: Humans

DID YOU KNOW?: Mammoths were named 'burrowing one' because when their bones were first found in Siberia, the local people thought that they were the remains of animals that lived underground.

COELODONTA

The woolly rhinoceros, *Coelodonta*, is one of the most familiar Ice Age mammals. It roamed the freezing northern plains, either on its own or in small family groups. Like the mammoth, it was well-adapted to cold conditions, even though its modern relatives live in tropical areas.

Coelodonta had many adaptations that helped keep it warm. It was covered in shaggy hair. It also had short legs and small ears, so these parts of its body did not get so cold.

The nose of the *Coelodonta* had a bony structure to support the weight of its horn, which was made of compacted hair. Both males and females had horns. They used them to push away snow, to reach the grass underneath.

ANIMAL FACTFILE

NAME: *Coelodonta* (hollow tooth)

PRONOUNCED: see-low-dont-ah

GROUP: Perissodactyl

WHERE IT LIVED: Northern Europe and Asia

WHEN IT LIVED: Early to Mid Quaternary Period (1.8 million to 20,000 years ago)

LENGTH: 3.3 metres

SPECIAL FEATURES: Two horns, one of which was 1 metre long

FOOD: Grass

MAIN ENEMY: Humans

DID YOU KNOW?: Early people hunted the woolly rhinoceros and drew pictures of it on cave walls in Central Europe.

SMILODON

The sabre-tooth cats were the main hunters of big animals during Quaternary times. A sabre is a curved sword, and that is exactly what *Smilodon*'s long front teeth were like. They could easily slash through thick skin and muscle. There were many types of sabre-tooth, and *Smilodon* was the biggest.

Smilodon's powerful jaw is obvious in this skull. The canine teeth were very long and used as killing weapons. They killed by slashing their prey, not biting it as modern cats do.

ANIMAL
FACTFILE

NAME: *Smilodon* (sabre toothed)

PRONOUNCED: smy-lo-don

GROUP: Machairodont group of the cats

WHERE IT LIVED: North America

WHEN IT LIVED: Early to Mid Quaternary Period (1.6 million to 11,000 years ago)

LENGTH: 1.5 metres

SPECIAL FEATURES: 15 cm canine teeth and strong neck muscles to drive them downwards with force

FOOD: Big mammals like elephants, horses and bison

MAIN ENEMY: None

DID YOU KNOW?: Many complete skeletons of *Smilodon* have been found in Los Angeles, USA. The animals became stuck in the tar pits there.

Smilodon was not a fast runner. Instead, it ambushed its prey and wounded it fatally. It would have then waited for the injured animal to bleed to death before eating it.

23

GIGANTOPITHECUS

The fierce *Gigantopithecus* could rear up to a great height, and bellow loudly. It was the biggest ape that ever lived. *Gigantopithecus* made its home in the forested foothills of the mountains of China.

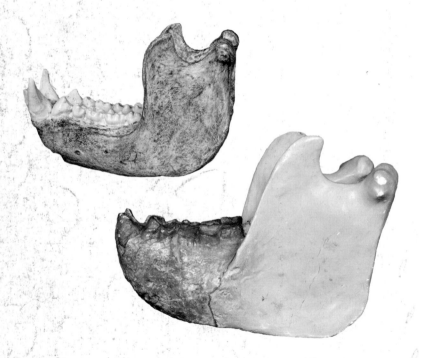

This picture shows a model of the jaw bone of *Gigantopithecus* (bottom) compared to the jaw bone of a gorilla (top). *Gigantopithecus* is very much bigger. All that scientists really know about *Gigantopithecus* are the size of its teeth. From the teeth, scientists can put together the appearance of the whole animal.

ANIMAL
FACTFILE

NAME: *Gigantopithecus* (giant ape)

PRONOUNCED: ji-gan-toe-pith-a-kuss

GROUP: Primate mammal

WHERE IT LIVED: China

WHEN IT LIVED: Late Tertiary Period to Early Quaternary Period (13 million to 500,000 years ago)

HEIGHT: 3 metres

SPECIAL FEATURES: Large teeth for chewing the tough mountain vegetation

FOOD: Bamboo and other plants

MAIN ENEMY: Not known

DID YOU KNOW?: *Gigantopithecus* was first discovered in 1935, when a German paleontologist found fossil teeth for sale in a Chinese medicine shop. He realised the teeth came from a primate that had never before been identified.

There is a theory that *Gigantopithecus* is still alive. Some people believe it is the Yeti, or abominable snowman, said to live in the Himalayas.

# AUSTRALOPITHECUS

Over millions of years, primitive monkey-like animals developed into the monkeys, apes and humans that live on Earth today. *Australopithecus* was an important member of this evolutionary line, being one of the first apes to walk on two legs. From upright apes like these, humans evolved.

The brain of *Australopithecus* was about a third of the size of a human brain. The teeth and the ear structure are more like those of an ape than a human.

Australopithecus lived on open plains, rather than in forests. It stood upright to see over tall grass. *Australopithecus'* hands were not used for walking on, like an ape, or for climbing, like a monkey. Instead its hands were used to grasp objects. However, its use of tools was not very advanced because its brain was still quite undeveloped.

ANIMAL FACTFILE

NAME: *Australopithecus* (southern ape)

PRONOUNCED: oss-trah-loh--pith-ek-us

GROUP: Hominid

WHERE IT LIVED: East and South Africa

WHEN IT LIVED: Late Tertiary Period to Early Quaternary Period (4.4 to 1.4 million years ago)

HEIGHT: 1.2 metres

SPECIAL FEATURES: The earliest ape to walk on two feet like a human

FOOD: Plants and animals

MAIN ENEMY: Big cats like lions and cheetahs

DID YOU KNOW?: There were several different species of *Australopithecus.* They were all smaller than modern humans.

HOMO

Homo is the group to which we belong. There have been several species. *Homo erectus* were the first humans to spread throughout the world from Africa, 100,000 years ago. Then came *Homo sapiens neanderthalensis* (Neanderthal man) and ourselves, *Homo sapiens* – the only surviving species.

This picture shows *Homo erectus*, one of our ancestors. *Homo erectus* used fire, and had tools made of stone, wood and bone.

Humans have two unique adaptations: large brains and mobile hands. This gives us the intelligence and the ability to use tools to make our lives better. In 4.5 billion years of evolution, there is no other species to develop the kind of intelligence that we have.

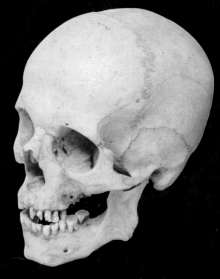

ANIMAL FAMILIES GLOSSARY

Artiodactyl — the group of even-toed hoofed mammals that include the deer, the sheep, the pigs and the camels. They have two toes on the foot, giving the "cloven hoof" appearance. They evolved later than the perissodactyls — the odd-toed hoofed mammals.

Glyptodont — the group of extinct xenarthran mammals that resembled gigantic armadillos. They lived in South America in the Quaternary Period, with one species known from North America.

Hominid — the group of primates that includes human beings and their immediate ancestors, as well as the chimpanzees, gorillas and orang-utans.

Machairodont — the group of sabre-toothed cats. The canine teeth were very long and used as killing weapons. They killed by slashing their prey, not biting it as modern cats do.

Marsupial — a major group of mammals that carry their young in pouches. Nowadays they are confined to Australia, except for the opossum of the Americas. In the Tertiary Period many of the hunting animals of South America as well as Australia were marsupials.

Perissodactyl — the group of odd-toed hoofed mammals. Modern forms include the horse, the rhinoceros and the tapir. They normally have either one toe or three on the foot. The other hoofed mammal group are the artiodactyls — the even-toed hoofed mammals.

Primate — the group of mammals that includes the lemurs, the monkeys, the apes and ourselves. Primates have hands and forward facing eyes.

Ratite — the group of flightless birds. Modern types include the emu and cassowary of Australia, the ostrich of Africa and the rhea of South America.

Varanid — the group of lizards that include the modern monitor lizards, such as the komodo dragon. Prehistoric forms include the swimming mosasaurs from the Cretaceous Period and the lion-sized lizards that lived in Australia during the Quaternary Period.

Xenarthran — the group of mammals that covers the anteaters, armadillos and sloths. They have always been confined to North and South America.